Surplus Federal Computers for Schools

An Assessment of the Early Implementation of E.O. 12999

Thomas K. Glennan, Jr., Walter S. Baer,
Susanna Purnell, Gwendolyn Farnsworth,
Gina Schuyler

Prepared for the
Office of Science and Technology Policy

Critical Technologies Institute

Preface

In April 1996, President Clinton signed Executive Order 12999, *Educational Technology: Ensuring Opportunity for All Children in the Next Century,* which was intended to promote the transfer of unneeded federal government computer equipment to schools. Government departments and agencies were required to develop implementation plans, which were to be submitted to the Office of Science and Technology Policy (OSTP) late in 1996.

In response to a request from Senator Patrick Leahy (D-VT), the White House Office of Science and Technology Policy (OSTP) asked RAND's Critical Technologies Institute (CTI) to assess the program's initial progress and provide recommendations for improvement.

This report examines the supply and distribution of surplus government computers and the implications for schools. It also looks at agencies' early experiences with E.O. 12999 and identifies lessons, from existing government programs and private-sector efforts, that might be applicable to federal efforts.

CTI was created in 1991 by an act of Congress. It is a federally funded research and development center operated by RAND. CTI's mission is to

- help improve public policy by conducting objective, independent research and analysis to support the Office of Science and Technology Policy in the Executive Office of the President of the United States;

- help decisionmakers understand the likely consequences of their decisions and choose among alternative policies; and

- improve understanding in both the public and private sectors of the ways in which technological efforts can better serve national objectives.

CTI research focuses on problems of science and technology policy that involve or affect multiple Executive Branch agencies, different branches of the U.S. government, or interaction between the U.S. government and states, other nations, or the private sector.

Inquiries regarding CTI or this document may be directed to:

Bruce Don

Director, Critical Technologies Institute

RAND

1333 H St., N.W.

Washington, D.C. 20005

Phone: (202) 296-5000

Web: http://www.rand.org.cti

Email: cti@rand.org

Contents

Figure

Tables

Summary

In April 1996, the President signed Executive Order (E.O.) 12999, *Educational Technology: Ensuring Opportunity for All Children in the Next Century.* The purpose of E.O. 12999 is to promote the transfer of unneeded federal government computer equipment to schools and educational nonprofit organizations. Government departments and agencies were required to develop implementation plans, which were to be submitted to the Office of Science and Technology Policy (OSTP) late in 1996.

Purpose and Research Approach

In response to a request from Senator Patrick Leahy (D-VT), OSTP asked RAND's Critical Technologies Institute (CTI) to assess the program's initial progress and provide recommendations for improvement.

In response, CTI staff conducted three tasks:

- Examined the potential supply of surplus government computers in relation to school needs

- Assessed agencies' early experiences with E.O. 12999, focusing on barriers to implementation

- Identified lessons and "best practices" from existing government programs and successful private-sector efforts that might be applied to overcome these barriers.

To do this, CTI gathered information on the number of computers that might be distributed from the 13 largest federal agencies and examined their implementation plans. We also conducted over 80 interviews with key agency personnel, private firms, nonprofit recycling organizations, state officials, schools, and school districts.

Characteristics of Federal Surplus Computers and Implications for Schools

The number of federal computers donated to schools is very uncertain. Based on interviews with government officials, we estimate that, in the last year, between 30,000 and 50,000 computers were donated either directly or through the Federal

Surplus Property Donation program.[1] In the future, donations could be significantly greater as a result of improved agency collection practices and greater use of refurbishing and upgrading services.

About a quarter of the government's approximately 2.1 million computers are replaced each year. Thus the number of computers potentially available for transfer is about 500,000 annually. However, most of these are not operable. Based on estimates given us by the private sector, we estimate that 10 to 35 percent of surplus computers are in good working order. If we use 20 percent as a reasonable figure, that would translate into approximately 100,000 working surplus computers available for donation from the federal government. Refurbishing and upgrading could double or triple the available number of working surplus computers and thus significantly increase the contribution of the federal donation program. Since public schools have acquired approximately 1 million computers annually for the past several years, effective implementation of E.O. 12999 has the potential to make a significant contribution to the installed base of computers in the nation's schools.

The uneven geographic distribution of the government computers influences the usefulness of this program to certain schools. Given the uneven distribution of government personnel throughout the United States and the federal regulations prohibiting agencies from packing and shipping computers,[2] the program has more potential for schools located in close proximity to federal installations than those at greater distances.

Implementing E.O. 12999: Major Barriers

We concentrated on the plans and experiences of the 13 agencies that hold over 90 percent of the government computers. We looked at two aspects of implementation: One concerns agency challenges, the second concerns the order itself.

Agency Challenges

For most agencies, the actual number of computers affected is small, and the donation effort itself is not central to the agency mission. Given these facts, a fairly predictable set of challenges emerged:

---

[1]Because there is no centralized reporting by agencies of automated data processing inventories, hard data on numbers of federal computers are difficult to obtain.

[2]Code of Federal Regulations 44 CFR 101-43.3, Utilization of Excess (Cost and Proceeds).

Lack of existing donation programs. Nine of the 13 agencies had no prior program. While those with experience built on previous programs, the others had to create new ones, including agency policy, guidelines, and documentation. However, the four agencies that did have existing programs house 55 percent of the government's computers, so this challenge is not as widespread as it might appear.

The program is not given high priority by the higher echelons. Most of the programs are housed in the property and inventory offices of the agency and get little attention from the upper-level managers.

No funds are authorized for carrying out the E.O. Given the era of government downsizing, most agencies treat this as an add-on task with little or no extra resources added.

Agency Concerns with the Executive Order

At the time of this study, agencies cited several problems and uncertainties about the intent and language of the E.O. itself:

The E.O. is unclear about its goals for school selection. The E.O. asks agencies to give preference to schools located in Empowerment Zones and Enterprise Communities (EZ/EC), but many agencies have existing competing programs that better reflect their missions and/or are perceived to make important contributions. Although the vague wording in the E.O. was intended to provide agencies with flexibility, the agencies are uncertain whether the E.O. allows them to continue to give priority to existing programs. The prohibition against agencies' shipping computers makes it even more difficult to transfer them to EZ/EC schools, which usually are located some distance from agency warehouses.

In the view of agencies, the E.O. does not adequately define "educational nonprofit organizations." Property managers, in particular, worry that such a general category of recipients increases the likelihood of fraud. Many agencies are handling the concern by dealing with schools only.

Although the E.O. suggests that the Federal Executive Boards (FEBs) assist agencies in identifying recipients and the Government Services Administration (GSA) could serve this function, neither has played this role. The FEBs have limited organizational support for such an effort. Although enthusiastic individual officials at the FEBs and GSA have been able to help identify recipients, there has been no consistent response.

While the E.O. mentions the use of nonprofit reuse and recycling programs, agencies have not done this. As noted below, recycling would add significant value to the program. However, agency program managers cite two barriers to using recyclers. First, the managers are wary of fraud and the difficulties of identifying legitimate recycling organizations. Second, agencies may transfer possession of the computers to a recycler only at the direction of the recipient institution or organization.

Federal policymakers have been monitoring and responding to these issues. A working group, centered in the Executive Office of the President (EOP), has been meeting regularly, consulting with the property managers, and exploring solutions to concerns raised by agencies. GSA sponsored a forum for all the agencies on implementation in March 1997. Policymakers are attempting to improve the outreach and selection of recipients through (1) developing a web site that is accessible to all federal agencies, on which schools can register technical needs; (2) encouraging the private sector to donate transportation of computers outside geographic areas; and (3) tasking GSA with clarifying the definitions accompanying the E.O.

Lessons from Private and Public-Sector Computer Donation Programs

The experiences of corporate and previous federal agency programs point to lessons for addressing some of the barriers to implementing the E.O.

Transferring equipment in good working order is essential. While some schools and districts have repair capabilities, the majority of schools cannot use donations unless they are complete working systems.

Donation programs must be managed. The most effective programs in the private and public sectors received active management support; had clear objectives, approaches, and organizational implications; and received adequate staff time and resources.

Refurbishing and upgrading provide more and better equipment for schools. Recyclers can increase the yield of working surplus computers and often warrantee and/or upgrade the computers transferred to schools at a much lower cost than for equivalent new machines. Private-sector experience indicates that refurbishing and upgrading can double the yield of working computers from a given surplus stock.

Recycling organizations offer advantages, but other approaches to refurbishing also seem feasible. While recycling organizations have the potential for operating on a larger scale, alternative models exist, such as vocational education programs run by school districts or other work-training approaches.

Conclusions and Recommendations

In our judgment, the early implementation of E.O. 12999 is proceeding in a reasonable manner. Inevitably, there are problems raised by the implementing agencies' disparate nature and by the geographic locations of the computers, but the agencies and the EOP appear to be working to deal with them.

As they proceed, the agencies and the EOP may want to consider the following four recommendations:

1. To address agency uncertainty and concerns, federal policymakers should clarify the status of preexisting transfer programs, the relative priority given to EZ/EC schools, and the definition of educational nonprofit organization.

2. To increase the yield of the program significantly, federal policymakers should explore ways to encourage the use of organizations capable of refurbishing and upgrading equipment, including addressing concerns about title transfer and the identification of acceptable recycling organizations.

3. To maximize the usefulness of the computers to participating schools, federal policymakers should continue to explore ways to support a more-informed selection process between the agencies transferring the equipment and the schools acquiring the equipment.

4. To make the program more beneficial to schools, federal agencies should ensure that only working computers configured in sets are transferred (unless transferring equipment to or via a recycling or refurbishing program).

While it is beyond the scope of E.O. 12999, the EOP should also consider the value of actions taken to enhance the usefulness of E.O. 12999 to donation and recycling programs more generally. For example, the web site currently under development for the federal government could be expanded to include private donors. In addition, the federal government might work with states to develop programs for certifying organizations providing refurbishing and upgrades.

Acknowledgments

In preparing this report, the Critical Technologies Institute staff talked with many people. The property managers and others responsible for the implementation of E.O. 12999, individuals in private firms, managers of recycling programs, and teachers and administrators in schools generously took the time to answer our questions. Frequently, they helped us to clarify and understand points in subsequent interviews. We are grateful for their assistance. The E.O. 12999 steering group—composed of Elisabeth Stock of the Office of the Vice President, Martha Livingston of the Office of Science and Technology Policy, Eric Macris of the Office of Management and Budget, and Martha Caswell of the General Services Administration—shared their plans and ideas with us as we began, then reviewed our report as we concluded. Within RAND, our colleagues Brent Keltner and David McArthur commented on earlier versions of this report.

1. Introduction

Increasingly, Americans view advancing technology as basic to a productive economy and link the acquisition of technology skills to the success of students moving into the workforce. Reflecting this view, the Clinton administration has launched a number of initiatives that promote integrating modern computer technology into every classroom, providing teachers with the professional development they need to use new technology effectively, connecting classrooms to the National Information Infrastructure, and encouraging the creation of excellent educational software. In support of these objectives, the administration issued Executive Order (E.O.) 12999, *Educational Technology: Ensuring Opportunity for All Children in the Next Century*, in April 1996, to promote the transfer of unneeded federal government computers and related equipment to elementary and secondary schools.

E.O. 12999 focuses on promoting the transfer of excess and surplus computers for education uses. The order, which supersedes a related E.O.,[1] requires federal agencies to protect "educationally useful federal equipment," and to transfer such equipment efficiently to schools and nonprofit organizations. It directs federal agencies to give preference to schools and nonprofit organizations located in the Federal Enterprise Communities and Empowerment Zones established under the authority of the Omnibus Reconciliation Act of 1993. The E.O. permits equipment to be initially conveyed to a nonprofit reuse or recycling program that upgrades it before it is transferred to the school or educational nonprofit organization that received title. The Federal Executive Boards (FEBs) are to help facilitate the transfer of educationally useful equipment from member agencies. The E.O. also encourages federal agency employees to volunteer time and expertise to help connect classrooms to the National Information Infrastructure, assist teachers in learning to use computers in teaching, and provide maintenance and technical support for the equipment transferred.[2] Agencies must report transfers annually under the E.O. to the General Services Administration (GSA).

---

[1] Executive Order 12821, *Improving Mathematics and Science Education*, was issued in 1992 and will be discussed briefly in Section 4.

[2] The implementation of the volunteer aspects of the order were not part of this study. The full text of E.O. 12999 is provided in Appendix A.

A key objective of the E.O. is to streamline the donation process by encouraging agencies to make direct transfers to schools rather than to use the more cumbersome alternative of donations through GSA and the State Agencies for Surplus Property. Direct transfer of excess computers by agencies, it was thought, would increase the number and timeliness of computer transfers to schools.

Purpose of the Study

In response to a request from Senator Patrick Leahy (D-VT), the Office of Science and Technology Policy (OSTP) asked RAND's Critical Technologies Institute (CTI) to assess the program's initial progress and provide recommendations for improvement. The purpose of the study was threefold:

1. to determine whether the size and condition of the federal computer surplus were adequate to justify such a large-scale donation effort

2. to get a picture of how federal agencies were coping with the E.O., in particular what kinds of barriers they might be encountering

3. to gain a clearer understanding of applicable federal experience with donation programs, as well as to draw lessons from private-sector successes that might aid in overcoming barriers to successful implementation.

Study Approach and Data Sources

In response, CTI staff conducted the following tasks:

- We estimated the potential supply and condition of surplus government computers.

- We reviewed agency implementation plans and interviewed relevant personnel to understand agencies' early experiences implementing E.O. 12999.

- We examined the experiences of a number of programs that refurbish and recycle computers before delivery to schools.

- Finally, we interviewed a limited number of school and district officials concerning their experiences with donated computer equipment, to gain some understanding of the schools' needs and perspectives.

The study was conducted over a three-month period extending from mid-December 1996 to early March 1997. This was a time of considerable change in many aspects of the environment we examined. The president's State of the Union and Budget messages reinforced and extended his administration's earlier emphasis on technology in K–12 schooling. State efforts to promote technology planning were beginning to have effects. A number of the state and private initiatives we examined had gained sufficient experience to begin adapting and extending their operations. Initial agency plans for implementing the E.O. had been completed just before we began our work.

There are virtually no reliable quantitative data describing the government's computer surplus programs. There are three primary reasons for this: First, personal computers and related equipment are comparatively low-cost items for which comprehensive record-keeping may not be implemented; second, they are grouped with other forms of automatic data processing (ADP) equipment for most management purposes; and third, they tend to become obsolete so quickly that, as a practical matter, they frequently are viewed as "consumables" like paper and pens rather than as durable pieces of capital equipment to be tracked and depreciated. This is true in both the private and public sectors.

As a consequence, this study relies heavily on interviews with individuals concerned with planning or managing donation programs or refurbishment and upgrade programs and with personnel in schools and school districts who have experience with receiving and using donated equipment. The approximate numbers of people interviewed are shown by category in Table 1.1. In many instances, we interviewed individuals several times to clarify information they had provided us.

We also reviewed key documents, including executive orders, public laws, and web site listings.

Table 1.1

Approximate Numbers of Interviews During Assessment of E.O. 12999

Responsibility of Interviewee	Interviewees
Senior policy officials	8
Federal agency officials	21
School district personnel	21
State agency personnel	3
Corporate donors	15
Recyclers and other nonprofits	15

NOTE: The numbers are approximate, and in some cases, interviewees were contacted more than once.

Organization of the Report

The remainder of the report is organized in four sections. Section 2 estimates the number, type, and condition of computers used by the government and the proportions of those that might be available for donation. These numbers are put in the context of overall public K–12 school acquisitions of computer equipment. While there is enormous uncertainty concerning the numbers, they suggest that a well-organized government program can potentially make useful contributions to the installed base of computers in American schools.

Section 3 contains the conclusions we drew from our interviews with key agency personnel and our review of the agency plans. An important finding is that personal computers tend to be concentrated in a small number of agencies. The largest of these have existing donation programs and are modifying them in accordance with the E.O. Smaller agencies also have had donation efforts, but these are highly decentralized, depend on the initiative of individual installations, and, often, depend on the efforts of a dedicated individual. For virtually all agencies, the responsibility for implementing the program rests with property managers and is necessarily a minor part of their responsibilities.

Section 4 presents lessons drawn from prior federal programs and from private-sector firms with successful donation programs. We felt that the experiences of these firms might be applicable to the federal program. Many of these firms found it more convenient to operate through an intermediary that refurbished and sometimes upgraded equipment. The intermediary also handled much of the distribution and often provided limited warrantees to recipients.

Section 5 contains our findings and recommendations.

2. Characteristics of Federal Surplus Computers and Implications for Schools

An assumption underlying E.O. 12999 is that the federal government possesses sufficient surplus computers to make a useful contribution to schools and other recipients. In this section, we test this assumption by examining the supply of federal surplus computers and the implications for public schools. We first estimate the available federal surplus and how much of the surplus stock is usable. We then discuss school needs in terms of annual computer purchases and the likely usefulness of the federal donations. Finally, we examine the geographic distribution of the federal stock in relation to where public school students are located. The latter issue is important because, as we note below, there is a geographic mismatch between the areas where federal computers are concentrated and the locations of schools designated as worthy candidates for donations.

Much of the information presented here represents educated guesses based on inputs from many individuals and organizations. Because federal agencies do not have to report components of ADP inventories to GSA, there is very little centralized information on personal computers from acquisition to their ultimate disposition. To develop the information provided in this section, we have synthesized information provided by individual agencies, market research firms, and private-sector recycling firms, as well as published government data.

The Supply and Operability of Surplus Federal Computers

How Many Surplus Computers Does the Federal Government Have?

The government owns approximately 2 million computers. We estimate that approximately 75,000 to 125,000 operative computers are available for donation each year. The federal government generates a sufficient number of usable surplus computers to account for a potential 7.5 to 12.5 percent of the computers schools acquire annually (see estimates of school acquisitions, below).[3]

---

[3]Our estimate of 2 million government-owned computers assumes that there are approximately 9 personal computers for every 10 civilian employees and one computer for every five uniformed

An unknown number of computers used by non–federal government employees are also potentially subject to requirements of the E.O. For example, interviews with Department of Energy (DoE) personnel indicate an additional 180,000 computers may be subject to the provisions of the E.O. because of the contractors that DoE supports.[4] Both the Department of Defense (DoD) and the National Aeronautics and Space Administration (NASA) also support extensive contractor-run organizations in which substantial proportions of computer equipment are purchased by the government and are thus subject to the provisions of the E.O.[5]

The lack of systematic policy regarding the application of the E.O. to computers in contractor facilities means the base from which surplus computers might be drawn is quite uncertain. For the rest of the discussion in this section, we will restrict ourselves to the computers used by government personnel, but the reader should bear in mind that agency implementation policies could increase these numbers somewhat.

How Many Surplus Computers Are in Operable Condition?

Because of rapid advances in technology, personal computers have limited useful lifetimes in many applications. Interviews with both agency and market-research personnel indicate that almost all computers purchased by the government are used to replace existing stocks rather than to increase the number of computers used. In 1996, the federal government replaced an estimated 27 percent of its computers.[6] The replacements, plus computers made available as a result of government downsizing, suggest that approximately 500,000 computers become surplus annually. However, the actual process by which computers work their way toward being surplus makes this figure a

---

military personnel. The ratios were obtained in interviews with the Colmar Group, a market research firm. Employment figures are taken from the 1997 Federal Budget. Another market research firm, IDC, in a separate interview, estimated the installed government base of personal computers to be 2.05 million.

[4]DoE supports approximately 120,000 contractor personnel in its national laboratories and other contractor-operated research facilities. Most of the computers used by these contractors are bought using funds from federal government contracts and thus are owned by the government. DoE has instructed these organizations to comply with the provisions of E.O. 12999 in disposing of surplus computing equipment. Because of the highly technical nature of the work of these installations, one DoE official estimated that there might be as many as 1.5 computers for every employee.

[5]In support of research reported in Section 4, we interviewed personnel at Lawrence Livermore Laboratories (largely supported by DoE) and the Jet Propulsion Laboratory (largely supported by NASA). Both indicated that they were implementing programs in accordance with the provisions of E.O. 12999. However, policies vary widely. Inquiries by both RAND and Office of Management and Budget (OMB) staff suggest that individual agency policies regarding government furnished equipment are varied and not centrally documented.

[6]Estimate was provided in an interview with IDC, a market research firm contracted by GSA to study government acquisitions.

significant overestimate of the number of operable computers that might be available for use by schools and nonprofit organizations.[7]

Interviews with personnel in both public and private organizations depict the somewhat chaotic progress of computer systems from installation to a point where they become surplus. Newly purchased systems are usually modern. As computer technology advances, new computers are bought for users needing improved performance. Computers that are replaced are passed on to the next level of users who, in turn, pass their old computers on to another set of users who either need less-capable computers or lack the clout to get better ones. Soon after leaving the desks of the initial users, computer systems begin to be "cannibalized": components, such as monitors, keyboards, memory or video boards, are used to repair or upgrade other computers. By the end of three or four years, a high proportion of the equipment can no longer can be called systems because they lack essential components.

Much of this flow of equipment is informal. A monitor from a slightly obsolete system may be used to replace another that has failed and whose repair is too costly or too difficult. Memory may be taken to upgrade another machine. A keyboard may be substituted for another that has failed. These actions are largely undocumented: The value of individual system components is too low to merit the cost of detailed tracking. As a result, at the end of three to four years, what emerges is an array of equipment that is usually "in pieces." Some of these pieces can be assembled into working systems. However, this assembly takes time and effort, because many of the pieces do not work.

We have been unable to obtain reliable estimates of the proportion of the surplus equipment that can be assembled into working sets. For example, at the low end, the East-West Foundation told us that about 5 percent of the computers they received could be immediately operated. A large school district suggested that perhaps a quarter of the systems were operative. One of the largest recyclers, the Detwiler Foundation, estimates that a third of the computers it receives from

---

[7]Property is declared *excess* when an internal screening reveals that the federal agency no longer has a need for the property to carry out their programs. They are required by law to report this property to GSA for transfer or disposal. When property is reported excess, GSA screens it with other federal agencies to ascertain if other federal requirements exist. GSA has the authority to transfer property from one federal agency that no longer needs it to another federal agency that has demonstrated a need. If no federal requirements are submitted, or if those submitted are not justified, GSA then determines the property to be *surplus* to all federal needs and available for disposal. Agencies are then allowed to transfer property directly to schools under E.O. 12999. If the agencies choose not to make a direct transfer, surplus computers are most often transferred through the Federal Surplus Donation Program, consisting of agencies from each state that ensure that the property is distributed fairly and equitably. If surplus real property is not disposed of through the state agencies, it is made available by competitive public sale.

businesses are operable.[8] To provide an estimate of the potential number of operating computers available for immediate donation, we will use a range of between 15 and 25 percent. This range, coupled with our earlier estimate that approximately 500,000 computers become available for donation each year, suggests that somewhere between 75,000 and 125,000 operative computers become available for donation each year.

The actual number of computers donated to schools by the federal government is very uncertain. Interviews with a variety of agency personnel suggest the number probably fell between 30 and 50 thousand in the past year. These computers are typically older machines. Both agency personnel and schools noted that, in the recent past, many schools complained that a high proportion of donated equipment consisted of old 286 machines that could not use advanced software or be conveniently networked. Obtaining data on this required more resources and time than were available for our study, but one regional GSA office was able to provide us with a record of transfers it handled between June 1996 and January 1997. Other anecdotal information suggests these percentages may be representative of the larger set of activities. These transfers included both GSA computers and computers from other agencies that turned their computers over to GSA for transfer. The data are shown in Table 2.1.

In summary, perhaps a half million computers become available for donation from federal agencies and departments each year, and of these, approximately 100,000 may be operable, although making them operable may require some effort in assembling sets of working parts. Most of these have been obsolete 286 PCs that cannot support either modern graphical interfaces, most current

Table 2.1

**Computer Donations by Philadelphia Regional
Office of GSA, June 1996–January 1997**

Computer Type	Number	Percent
286	227	55
386	168	41
486	17	4
Total	412	100

NOTE: About 70 percent of these machines were delivered to two Philadelphia high schools that served as distribution points and sometimes repaired and/or upgraded the machines.

---

[8]The Detwiler figure is probably high relative to that for federal surplus computers. Detwiler will not accept some low-end computers and components. A recycler's estimate of donated equipment that is functional "as is" will depend on its definition of "functional," minimum standards for donations, and the sources of donations.

educational software, or routine networking.[9] In the future, of course, the numbers of 286 PCs will sharply decline.

Surplus Computers Are Concentrated in a Few Agencies

Finally, an important characteristic of federally owned computers is that they are concentrated among a few government agencies. These agencies own large stocks of computers primarily because they have the largest numbers of personnel. Some agencies, such as DoD, DoE, and NASA have additional needs for computers because they must furnish computers to their associated contractor personnel. The agency mission also drives their need for computers. For example, the Forest or Park Services are likely to have lower ratios of computers to personnel, whereas technical agencies, such as NASA, DoE, and the R&D components of DoD, probably have higher ratios. While an accurate count of federal computers requires taking account of these differences, lack of available information on those differences prevents us from doing so. In the case of the three agencies most affected by computer needs for contractors and agency missions (DoD, DoE, and NASA), the individual agencies provided us with estimates of their computer base. Assuming that other agency computer stocks were largely driven by their personnel population, we used a ratio of 9 computers for every 10 employees to determine their computer base.

Figure 2.1 displays the concentration of computers among agencies using our simple assumptions. It suggests that about two thirds of the computers are concentrated in three agencies. The largest agencies that perform more technical and scientific tasks, such as DoD, DoE, and NASA, had the most active agencywide programs at the time of the issuance of E.O. 12999.

The implementation of the E.O. must recognize this wide disparity in agency size and be structured in ways that allow the larger and more technical agencies to operate programs that match their operational structures, needs, and histories, while helping the smaller agencies to comply with the E.O. at a minimum of cost and effort.[10]

---

[9]Most, but not all, of the available equipment consists of IBM-compatible PCs rather than computers made by the Apple Corporation. In 1995 and 1996, QED Inc. estimated that approximately 39 percent of the installed K–12 base of computers were IBM compatible. Thus, in addition to the obsolete character of donated federal machines, most are incompatible with what has been the dominant brand of machine in the education market. However, recent sales data suggest that Apple is losing market share in the K–12 computer market.

[10]This point is discussed more thoroughly in the next section, where we deal with individual agency plans.

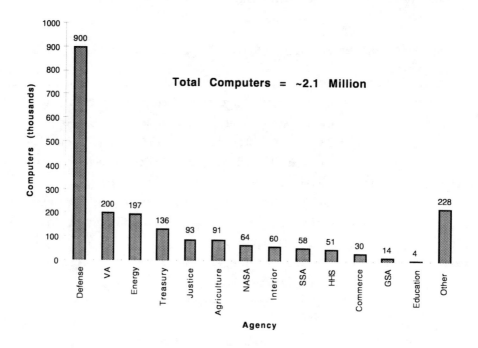

Figure 2.1—Estimated Distribution of Computers Among Agencies and Departments[11]

Implications for Public Schools

How Many Computers Do Public Schools Acquire?

According to Quality Educational Data (QED), a firm that specializes in tracking educational technology in schools, public schools acquire about one million computers a year. In the last few years, a significant proportion of these have replaced older and less able computers, such as the venerable Apple IIs. Thus, the estimated 75,000 to 125,000 operating computers available each year from the federal government would represent a useful component of the number acquired annually.

It is illuminating to look at this supply in the context of overall national educational stocks and potential needs. QED estimates that in 1995 and 1996, about 4.4 million computers were used for instruction in the public schools,

---

[11]DoD, DoE, and NASA figures are based upon agency estimates. All other agency estimates are based upon a computer-to-employee ratio of 9:10 and employment figures from 1997 budget.

serving about 44 million students. In other words, the ratio of students per computer was about 10 to 1.[12] If all schools could reach a ratio of 5 students for each computer, a figure often cited as a requirement, the nation's schools would have to acquire about 4.5 million computers in addition to replacing broken and obsolete machines.[13] The donation of federal surplus computers could therefore make only a small contribution to improving the student-computer ratio. However, combining an expanded federal program with state and private programs could significantly increase the contribution.

How Well Does the Prospective Surplus Stock Fit School Needs?

Two points emerged from our interviews with schools about their computer needs and the usefulness of donated equipment: The first concerned the issue of functionality, the second the issue of computer age and quality.

The functionality issues were a common theme in interviews with schools and school districts. Problems schools experienced included incompatibility with district technology, lack of maintenance capabilities, and costs associated with replacing missing components, software, licenses, and training. Although a majority of computer donations in the past have been nonfunctional, schools expressed a reluctance to turn down unwanted equipment for political reasons. The schools fear their rejection of public or private equipment might cause negative community relations and possibly discourage further donations.

Although schools can find uses for older computers still in functional condition, there are important downsides to heavy reliance on older donated computers by schools. Low-end computers, such as 286s, are inadequate for connection to the Internet. Modern educational and business software is normally written for use by relatively modern, high-performance systems. While some of this emphasis on modern high-power equipment is used to implement features of little educational value, much of the reason for concentration on high-power machines is to gain the benefits of modern graphic environments, which make the programs easier to use, more engaging, and more flexible. For this reason, the

---

[12]The ratios vary widely among states. Florida has the fewest students per computer, with a ratio of 5.9 to 1. At the other end of the spectrum is Delaware, with a ratio of 15.3 to 1. These data were taken from the table titled Educational Technology by State found at QED's web site, http://www.qeddata.com/.

[13]Of the 4.4 million currently in schools, QED data suggest about 43 percent are what QED terms multimedia computers, which they define as "including all computers which are Macintosh or have a 386 or higher processor and are capable of supporting CD-ROM drives and/or sound and video cards."

software industry and its spokesmen at the Software Publishers Association (SPA) have taken a relatively negative stand on the value of donation programs.[14]

While software publishers have an obvious interest in seeing that schools have significant stocks of modern computers capable of using the software they develop, the SPA makes important points. For many educational applications, computers that are normally available through direct donations are inadequate. For other applications—e.g., learning keyboarding skills or simple text processing—older computers and software may be quite adequate. A school and a school system should have a clear sense of its technology needs and a strategy for meeting those needs. In the absence of such a strategy or plan, it may end up with computers it cannot effectively use at the same time it lacks the technical capability to capitalize on important benefits of modern software or networking.

Access to Donated Computers May Be Unequal

As a general rule, computer donations or transfers to schools are made at minimum cost to the donating agency. In many cases, schools pick them up from warehouses or storage areas. In some cases, government volunteers have delivered them. The comparatively low value of the computers, coupled with administrative regulations, means that almost all computers are distributed to schools that are relatively close to the government facilities where the computers were originally used. This means that schools across the nation have differential access to the computers based upon the distribution of government employment.

The E.O. provides no funding for agencies to pack and ship surplus computers.[15] Therefore, if equity in distribution is important, costs will need to be incurred to increase equity in the donation of equipment. Table 2.2 provides a rough portrayal of the estimated distribution of government computers compared to the distribution of students. Virginia, Maryland, Alaska, and Hawaii are estimated to have more than eight installed federal personal computers per hundred students (as does the District of Columbia). Most states have between two and six federal computers per hundred students.

The implication of data presented in this table is that, in the absence of specific directions and perhaps funding for shipping, schools that are closer to

---

[14]"Donated Computers: An Educator's Guide," 1996. This document comprises an "SPA Position Paper" and "An Educator's Checklist" regarding school acquisition of used computers. The document is available on SPA's web site: www.spa.org/project/educator.htm.

[15]44CFR 101-43.3, Utilization of Excess (Cost and Proceeds) of the Code of Federal Regulations, prohibits agencies from packing and shipping equipment to schools.

Table 2.2

Ratio of Federal Personal Computers per 100 Students (by State)[16]

More than 6	4 to 6	2 to 4	Less than 2
Dist. of Columbia	New Mexico	Tennessee	Minnesota
Hawaii	Colorado	Mississippi	Iowa
Maryland	Georgia	California	Wisconsin
Virginia	Montana	Nevada	Michigan
Alaska	North Dakota	Nebraska	
	Alabama	Oregon	
	Oklahoma	Texas	
	Washington	Delaware	
	Wyoming	Florida	
	Utah	West Virginia	
	South Dakota	Idaho	
	Kentucky	Louisiana	
	Missouri	New Jersey	
	Arizona	Vermont	
	North Carolina	Illinois	
	Rhode Island	Arkansas	
	South Carolina	Ohio	
	Kansas	New York	
	Pennsylvania	Indiana	
	Massachusetts	Connecticut	
	Maine	New Hampshire	

concentrations of government employment will have better access to surplus computers than those that are more remote from such employment.

Summary

The analysis in this section supports several important conclusions.

1. The federal government generates a sufficient number of usable surplus computers to make a useful contribution to the technology base in American schools.

2. A large proportion of the surplus computers are not in condition to be used and must either be refurbished or upgraded to be useful in school settings.

3. A small number of agencies account for a high proportion of federal government employment and therefore stocks of personal computers. Their policies will have the largest effect on the success of the goals of E.O. 12999.

---

[16]This chart is constructed using ratios of computers per employee together with numbers of federal and military personnel per state (provided by the Office of Personnel Management) to estimate the number of federal computers in a state. The numbers of students in a state are taken from the Digest of Educational Statistics for 1995. The chart does not reflect computers subject to E.O. 12999 that are in the hands of contractors.

4. The geographic distribution of equipment is not evenly matched with the distribution of potential recipients. If equity in distribution is of great importance, costs will need to be incurred to increase equity in the donation of equipment.

5. Because the technology advances so quickly in the educational technology field, donated equipment will have limited roles to play in most schools. Effective technology plans that guide the selection and use of equipment are important.

3. Agency Responses to E.O. 12999: Progress and Barriers

In this section, we assess agencies' early experiences with E.O. 12999, focusing on barriers to implementation. The section characterizes agency progress and challenges to date and highlights issues and uncertainties regarding the intent and interpretation of the E.O. It also explores the role of intermediary agencies in promoting the distribution of surplus computers.

Because most of the federal surplus computers come from relatively few agencies, this report gathered data on 13 agencies that account for an estimated 90 percent of the federal computers. These included ten executive departments, as well as the Social Security Administration, GSA, and NASA.[17]

The current E.O. applies across all federal agencies, most of which had no experience creating an agencywide donation program.[18] The lack of experience with this kind of program contributed to uncertainty and hesitancies about implementing some activities encouraged by the E.O. An earlier E.O. (12821) articulated a similar set of donation goals, but applied only to agencies with relevant missions, so that most government agencies did not respond.

Agency Challenges

Based on the information gathered on the 13 federal agencies, the implementation plans describe modest programs. The following conclusions characterize the overall response of these agencies.

The E.O. had the effect of promoting wider agency participation. In this study, 9 of the 13 agencies studied had no previous agency-sponsored program for transferring computers to schools and so were creating one for the first time. Most agencies make direct transfers to schools and other qualifying recipients rather than transferring the property through GSA and the State Agencies for Surplus Property (SASPs) to a recipient. This approach streamlines the process

---

[17]Sources of information included interviews with program planners and/or examination of E.O. 12999 implementation plans submitted to the Office of Science and Technology Policy for the following departments: Defense, Veterans Affairs, Energy, Treasury, Justice, Agriculture, Interior, Health and Human Services, Commerce, and Education.

[18]Within agencies, some facilities or bureaus may have had school partnerships or other local programs, but this was not done under the guidance of the agency headquarters.

and takes less time, making it less likely that the equipment will degrade further.[19] The direct-transfer approach, however, means more work for the agency, which must identify a recipient, arrange the pick-up of equipment, and transfer the deed. Getting most of the responding agencies to take this approach indicates that the E.O. has resulted in a much wider effort than previously existed. Of the 13 agencies examined, only one was using the GSA donation program.

If federal agencies are demonstrating wider participation in responding to E.O. 12999 as compared to the previous orders, some appear to have shallower levels of commitment. Several factors contribute to this response. First, although most view the program as contributing toward improved education, these agencies see little or no connection between the program and their own mission or function. In addition, current incentives—such as the emphasis on downsizing—and the small size of the surplus generated by most agencies work against a significant commitment.

There is limited involvement within the agency beyond the program managers. Once the program is in place, there is little or no review and participation on the part of agency leadership and policymakers. The programs primarily are housed in the property and inventory offices of the agency. In 7 of the 13 agencies, responsibility has been assigned to those offices, a figure that probably underrepresents this tendency, because the remaining agencies allow bureaus or local facilities to assign management of the program.

A relatively low level of effort is assigned to the program. In almost all the agencies, the program is administered as an add-on responsibility to an existing job. The incentive is to make this a minimal process, one that does not require too much time or effort to locate recipients and make the transfer. This tends to support selecting recipients on a first come, first served basis with equipment transferred "as is" and no further responsibility once it leaves the warehouse. Since agencies are prohibited from using their own resources in delivering the

---

[19]The 1992 Stevenson-Wydler Act amendment, enacted by Public Law 102-245, authorized federal departments, agencies, or laboratories to make direct transfers of excess research equipment to educational institutions or nonprofit organizations. Title to the property passes to the recipient at the time of the direct transfer and, unlike most transfers of excess Federal property, does not require approval from GSA. In contrast, under the Federal Property and Administrative Services Act of 1949, surplus personal property may be donated to public agencies for public purposes and to certain nonprofit tax-exempt activities. Under the 1949 act, property can be donated through the GSA donation program or by using expedited education-related transfers, which involves notifying GSA of a recipient selection and then having GSA transfer the property to the State Agencies for Surplus Property (SASPs) for distribution. Under this method, the title is conditional; the donee must place the equipment into use within the first year and then use it at least one more year for its intended purpose to be in compliance.

equipment, the "can't pack, can't ship" policy further reinforces limited involvement in the process.

Challenges Related to the Executive Order

In addition to program placement and level of effort within the agencies, the program has also been influenced by perceived ambiguities in the E.O. itself. These mostly affect identifying and selecting the program recipients. The following points summarize key concerns:

The relationship between programs under the E.O. and prior programs is unclear. Because the order gives "particular preference to schools and nonprofit organizations located in Federal empowerment zones and enterprise communities," and also specifies that this order supersedes the previous E.O., some agencies view the order as conflicting with already established programs. Agencies are particularly concerned about aspects of the E.O. that conflict with existing programs more directly related to their mission, such as the Public Health Service's program with the Indian Tribal Councils, or the Department of Labor's giving priority to transferring computers to the Job Corps Centers. In addition, an agency or a section of any agency may have prior partnerships with specific schools or programs. Finally, there is some concern about programs established under the preceding E.O. 12821, especially when it includes elements not sanctioned by the current order.[20]

The intent behind preferences for EZ/EC schools has not been well understood. The federal agencies also have had trouble understanding the intent of giving preference to schools located in EZ/ECs.[21] In part, the issue is whether these schools take precedence over every other applicant regardless of preexisting program ties or other factors. But agency policymakers also thought the intent of the provision was to target needy schools.[22] They viewed the

---

[20]There are two major concerns about such programs: They provide a wider array of donations under the rubric of "research equipment," and E.O. 12821 authorizes the use of employee time to work on such projects rather than volunteering nonwork time. Agencies within DoD have already threatened to terminate programs unless the "shall supersede Executive Order 12821" language is removed from E.O. 12999. There is some disagreement about the consequences of this language, since federal policymakers believed the language of E.O. 12999 protected such programs.

[21]Empowerment Zones (EZ) and Enterprise Communities (EC) are urban and rural grantees under the 1993 Omnibus Budget Reconciliation Act. Community members and federal agencies together develop a strategic plan toward economic, community, and human-resource development. The grants are used to leverage investment in the community. There are 15 urban and rural EZs located in ten states, and 90 ECs throughout the country.

[22]There is some evidence that the EZ/EC schools are not necessarily the most poorly resourced schools, especially in terms of technology. Schools serving a high-poverty population receive Title I funds that often are put toward technology. Moreover, state and local initiatives also provide extra resources. For example, schools in the rural Kentucky Highlands EZ have benefited from a strong state-level technology initiative that has stressed equity for the more poorly resourced schools.

requirement as implying the agencies should pay more attention to making equitable disbursements from the program. The E.O.'s reporting requirement was viewed by many agency program planners as a way of avoiding a concentration of equipment in a few favored schools.

Beyond these concerns are the practical considerations of making connections with the EZ/EC schools. Since the zones and communities themselves do not always coincide with school district boundaries, agencies eventually were provided lists of all the schools located in the EZs.[23] In addition, the program tends to serve nearby schools because the agencies are not allowed to ship the equipment.[24] Although some of the EZs located in cities may be near federal warehouses, the rural EZ/ECs are not; federal facilitators for both programs cite transportation as a major barrier to the EZ/EC schools using the program. All the examples we learned of computer transfer to schools in these zones and communities involved volunteer transportation.

"Educational nonprofit organizations" were not clearly defined. If agencies are unsure of meeting the intent of the E.O. in terms of targeting EZ/EC schools, they are having even greater difficulty determining the eligibility of educational nonprofit organizations. Agency program managers are wary of fraud and the difficulty of identifying nonprofit institutions that hide internal profits or that do not meet the E.O.'s intent.

Agencies have addressed the concern in several ways. Some have incorporated the GSA-approved definition of educational nonprofits and/or required the applicant to submit proof of Internal Revenue Service certification. The DoD has gone to the expense of purchasing the list of qualifying institutions from the Internal Revenue Service, but the list is not necessarily current. Others also use the language of the E.O.: The nonprofit organization must be "community-based." Yet, even with these qualifiers, agency program managers indicated they would want to investigate the applicant to assure legitimacy. Some agencies have simply eliminated nonprofits as program recipients. Others indicated that, as long as the list of applying schools exceeds the existing surplus, there is no need to deal with applications from nonprofit institutions. No matter what the

---

Although these schools received computers from the E.O. 12999 program, they were of very limited use because the low-end surplused equipment could not be integrated into the schools' more sophisticated network.

[23]A listing of schools located in the 15 empowerment zones can be found on the HUD web site: The address is: www.hud.gov/ezeclist.html

[24]In most of the implementation plans, the program outreach concentrates on local contacts or advertising. At least one agency program manager stipulates that recipients should be within a day's car ride.

approach, agency program planners and directors cite the need for more guidance in identifying this category of recipients.

The Roles of GSA and the Federal Executive Boards

E.O. 12999 suggests that the GSA and the FEBs can help agencies identify recipients. Experience has been mixed.

General Services Administration

The E.O. suggests that GSA could provide assistance in matching agency excess equipment with specific schools. The willingness of GSA to take on this role varies by location. Headquarters GSA is not interested in this role itself, but some regional offices of agencies are using the GSA screening system for all federal excess equipment to play the role of matchmaker, particularly in the New England and mid-Atlantic regions. In both these areas, the FEBs have promoted interagency use of the GSA services. The result in the mid-Atlantic region has been the transfer of over 330 computers since May 1996, with the bulk of the excess going to a vocational education repair and recycling program located in Philadelphia. The New England program has resulted in weekly awards of computers to different schools in the region.

Federal Executive Boards

Although the E.O. encourages the FEBs to act as intermediaries between agencies and schools, the organizational structure and nature of the boards makes it difficult for them to fulfill this function. As a body that promotes interagency communication within the region, an FEB has a staff of no more than two or three people. It receives direction annually from the Office of Personnel Management, but this primarily consists of a list of policy areas targeted for emphasis that year. Individual FEBs select from the list and develop several projects to work on during the year. The selection and the response often depend on the personality and interests of the chairman, who in turn often relies on the resources of the agency from which he or she comes to accomplish the task.

Within these limitations, some FEBs have played a role in the distribution of computers to schools, identifying recipients for the program and coordinating donations across a number of agencies. The Alamo FEB, for example, established an interagency council several years ago to provide resources to needy schools. The council conducts an annual survey of the computer needs of schools, ranks the schools by the ratio of students to computers, and uses that ranking to coordinate the distribution of computers from the military bases in the area to the schools with the highest ratios. The Baltimore FEB also acts as a middleman, putting agency property managers in touch with school-district property managers.

In general however, the organizational structure of the FEBs appears inadequate to fulfill an intermediary function. There is no consistency in the response across FEBs, and most view the more formalized program of the Alamo FEB as too complicated and extensive an effort for the FEB structure. Finally, FEBs change their focus and their chairmen over time.

Those knowledgeable with the operation of FEBs suggest that a more useful role may be taking the opportunity of interagency meetings to compare best practices and experiences and to promote enthusiasm and support at higher levels within the agencies through presentations and examples of successes.

Use of Nonprofit Organizations to Refurbish and Upgrade Computers

The E.O. mentions using nonprofit reuse or recycling organizations to repair and upgrade equipment in the course of the transfer of computers to the schools. Generally, agency planners and program managers have little interest in dealing with such organizations. They worry about establishing the legitimacy of such organizations and voice additional qualms if the recycler charges the school a fee. While concerned about fraud, program policymakers and administrators said they would be more likely to work with such organizations if approved lists were available. Otherwise, they feel they would have to investigate the legitimacy of each possible organization, an enterprise that would involve more effort than most agency program managers are willing to expend.

Agencies cannot transfer the computer titles to a recycler; they can only transfer them to a school or nonprofit education organization. Thus, the agencies are comfortable dealing with vocational education programs that work with computer repair. Transfer to such programs is straightforward because the recipient is a school or school system and the equipment is being used for educational purposes. Such transfer also reduces the agencies' need to assemble operable systems, since the equipment can benefit the vocational education program no matter what the condition.

Activities of Federal Policymakers

Federal policymakers are well aware of agency concerns. A working group including members of the Office of the Vice President (OVP), OSTP, GSA, and OMB has been meeting weekly to monitor the implementation and respond to agency concerns. In December 1996, the group began meeting with ten program managers from some of the larger agencies to get their feedback on issues related to the E.O. The working group is supporting development work on a World Wide Web site that would eventually serve as a "one-stop shopping place" for the educational community to request and arrange donations of federal government computing equipment. The working group used the program managers as sounding boards for developing the details of the web site. The working group has also responded to agency questions, especially in providing reassurance that the E.O. was not intended to eliminate previous programs.[25] OVP has been exploring ways to enlist private-sector help in providing transportation of donated equipment from agency warehouses to schools.

GSA has also been providing advice and guidance. The agency created a pamphlet after the E.O. was issued to provide some guidance and points of contact. In addition, GSA sponsored a March 1997 workshop on the E.O. for all the federal agencies. Workshop participants contributed ideas for improving the design of the developing web site. In addition, GSA was charged with developing more detailed definitions as part of the implementation guidance. The working group believes this may help clarify some of the uncertainties surrounding the order.

Summary

Given that, for most agencies, the numbers of computers to be donated by individual installations are small and that the plan was for a new add-on effort, we view the responses by most agencies as reasonable and appropriate. The larger agencies and departments with established programs have moved to bring these programs into broad conformance with the terms of the E.O.

The implementation of the E.O. will always vary among agencies, reflecting the individual character and location of each agency and the history of its donation programs. While the largest agencies can reasonably establish their own programs, most of the 59 participating government agencies have such a small

---

[25]There has been concern among some managers that only written guidance will guarantee the continuation of some already established programs.

amount of surplus equipment that they often will be best served by using intermediaries, such as GSA or the FEBs.

The current working group effort to establish a multiagency web site may well assist agencies in implementing the E.O., especially after schools generally become more proficient in using the web. However, the working group should continue to assess the adequacy of efforts to provide schools and school systems with knowledge concerning the availability of equipment for donation.

In addition, we recommend the following:

- Individual agencies should contribute to the quality and reputation of the program by making a commitment to transfer computers as operable, working systems, except when it is clear that they will be refurbished or upgraded.

- The working group and the GSA should continue to address agency concerns about the clarity and intent of the language of the E.O.

- The working group should seek ways to encourage greater use of organizations that refurbish and upgrade computers. Perhaps there are ways to tap the knowledge of state agencies in this area. Working through states, it may be possible to identify reputable organizations that schools may use. Finally, it may be desirable to seek authority to permit the direct transfer of computers to such organizations.

4. Lessons from Past Government Donation Programs and the Private Sector

Because the implementation of E.O. 12999 was still in progress at the time of this study, we examined experiences with past computer donation for lessons learned. We conducted interviews with ten corporations, four federal agencies, and eight foundations and other nonprofit organizations to explore why and how the computer donation programs were run and any changes that were made as a result of their experiences.[26] In addition, we also gathered information on the programs and reactions of two state education agencies and several large school districts.[27] The following provides a general summary of the approaches and circumstances that contribute to effective donor programs based on the experiences of these corporations and federal agencies. A key finding is that the use of intermediaries, such as nonprofit recyclers and refurbishers, greatly enhances that effectiveness. Appendix B provides a more detailed look at several recycling organizations, as does an accompanying study.[28]

Experiences of Selected Federal Transfer Programs

There are several examples of past federal programs that encourage agencies to transfer programs to schools or educational institutions. These programs are the products of previous laws, executive orders, and general practice and have often reflected support of administration policy. A series of executive orders, for example, demonstrated administration commitment to education and equity issues by encouraging transfer of surplus research equipment to minority higher-

---

[26]Corporations and industry associations interviewed included Ameritech, Apple Computer, Eli Lilly, Hughes Electronics, IBM, Intel, Microsoft, Pacific Bell, Software Publishers Association, and Walt Disney Company. The foundations and other nonprofit organizations included Computer Recycling Center, Detwiler Foundation, East-West Educational Development Foundation, Gifts In Kind, Joint Venture Silicon Valley, Lazarus Foundation, Los Angeles Educational Partnership, and National Cristina Foundation. The federal agencies were programs run by the DoD, DoE, NASA, and the Immigration and Naturalization Service.

[27]State agencies and school districts included the California Computer Refurbishing Fund; Central Indiana Educational Service Center; Los Angeles County Office of Education; Los Angeles Unified School District; San Diego County Office of Education; San Diego Unified School District; State of California, Office of Educational Technology; Baltimore City Public Schools; and Washington, D.C., Public Schools.

[28]Walter S. Baer and Gwendolyn Farnsworth, *Computer Donations to Schools, Review of Non-Federal Programs*, DRU-1605-OSTP, forthcoming.

24

education institutions.[29] Within agencies, there are examples of local facilities and programs participating in Adopt-a-School or partnership-in-education programs, a volunteer activity that sometimes included some transfer of computers.

One of the most relevant past experience has come from the donation programs generated by E.O. 12821, *Improving Mathematics and Science Education* in Support of the National Education Goals, issued in 1992. This order asked agencies to assist elementary and secondary schools in emphasizing math and science by donating education-related equipment. Issued at the end of the Bush administration but implemented by the current administration, the program was viewed as a way to leverage federal resources in support of the national goals for education and tasked only agencies with math- and science-related missions to respond to the order.

In government, organizational and resource support characterized past successful programs. For example, in response to the orders encouraging transfers of research equipment to minority institutions of higher education, the DoE established a well-defined program targeting specific colleges and universities. The agency committed the necessary resources, providing intended recipients with program training and electronic access to relevant excess property. The DoD responded to E.O. 12821 by establishing uniform application procedures and transfer policies for K–12 schools across the civilian and military sectors of the department. Those responsible for the program courted agency leadership support and set up a coordinating group to assist in implementation. The program itself was run by a small office staff established solely for that purpose.

Several characteristics of these two federal programs contributed to their success. These agencies have the largest computer inventories and could therefore field significant transfer programs. Both agencies perceived that the program was relevant to their missions. The donations to the science departments of minority colleges fit the research orientation of DoE laboratories. The DoD leadership viewed the school donation program as contributing to the quality of future recruits for the armed services. In addition, commanders of local facilities saw the program as contributing to good community relations. The program's credibility in the eyes of the top echelons contributed to the marshaling of the necessary resource support, including dedicated administrative positions.

---

[29]These include E.O. 12876, *Historically Black Colleges and Universities*; E.O. 12900, *Hispanic Association of Colleges and Universities*; and E.O. 13021, *Tribal Colleges and Universities*.

Finally, it should be noted that not all successful examples come from the large agencies with related missions. There are examples of smaller agencies tailoring the program to their capacity using objectives other than the agency mission. These give some hint of the decentralized nature of the federal experience. For example, Immigration and Naturalization Service headquarters piloted a well-regarded donation program for the agency based on a partnership with a local needy school. The facility transferred computers to the school, but agency members first formed a joint steering committee with school leaders to work out a technology plan and to identify needed equipment. Agency volunteers provided a number of support tasks under the larger umbrella of the school partnership. As in the other examples, the program had high-level support, dedicated resources, and well-defined objectives and approach.

Direct Donations by Private Firms to Schools

Corporations established computer donation programs for a number of reasons that often fell under the general banner of supporting educational improvement. However, this actually translated into a variety of sometimes competing goals, including helping local schools that employees' children attended, improving the computer training of students who would become the firm's future workforce, or improving education in general. Interestingly, few donors cited economic benefits as a driving force in establishing such programs.[30] Because most computers have been fully depreciated by the time they are donated, tax deductions provide little incentive.[31] A fairly universal goal of these programs, however, was to contribute to the firm's community relations by gaining goodwill from computer gifts to schools.

In establishing donation programs, corporations typically started by giving used computers directly to selected local schools and other nonprofit organizations. However, experience soon proved that running a successful program often included unanticipated demands. First, many corporations did not foresee the time and effort required to communicate with recipients, arrange transfers, and choose among competing candidate schools. Direct donors often found themselves having to prioritize a waiting list of dozens to hundreds of potential recipients. The most successful responded with clear objectives and approaches that balanced competing goals, established a process for recipient outreach and selection, and defined the program boundaries and resources.

---

[30]This proved to be true even of the hardware and software suppliers. These firms preferred to donate or sell new products to schools at a discount than to give used ones.

[31]A few states have enacted special tax credits for computer gifts to schools. In Indiana, state tax credits appeared to be an important motivation for corporate donations.

The most effective donation programs tended to be those with visibility inside the organization and active support from senior management. Generally, programs managed within a corporate education or community-relations program had greater visibility and commitment than those run by a technical or property-management department.

In addition to defining the program management within the corporation, firms found schools to be unsophisticated technology users who needed a great deal of support. Schools usually lacked the capacity to deal with computers delivered "as is." Donors began hearing complaints that the machines were inoperable or lacked the necessary operating software. In some instances, the computers operated for a while and then malfunctioned. While many school districts provided maintenance services, donated computers often fell outside district maintenance contracts. Schools were then left to maintain donated equipment themselves.

Corporate donors demonstrated several responses to these concerns. Some firms encouraged employees to volunteer their own time to install and repair donated computers and train teachers to use and maintain them.[32] Facilities with local school partnerships sometimes included such activities in the context of this wider business-school relationship. However, many firms, while willing to donate computer equipment, did not want their programs to become long-term maintenance and support services for schools. Computer repair, maintenance, and training were expensive (and unbudgeted) problems for corporations. Facing their own budget pressures, firms were unable to warrantee their gifts or provide computer support to the recipients. As a result, some firms began viewing donation programs as potential generators of ill, rather than good, will.

Computer Recycling and Intermediary Organizations

Many private firms addressed the concerns that arose from direct donation programs by completely changing their approaches and donating used equipment through third-party, nonprofit computer recyclers or intermediary organizations.[33] A typical recycler receives donated equipment; checks to see

---

[32]Hughes Electronics Corporation headquarters, for example, sponsored a program in which employee volunteers spent their lunch hours inspecting and, where necessary, repairing surplus computers before they were donated. Volunteers would then work with teachers and others at recipient schools to make sure the computers remained in good working order. Often this was part of an ongoing program of corporate assistance to Hughes' partnership schools. Unfortunately, the program ended in 1996 when Hughes Electronics outsourced most of its computer operations to another firm and consequently no longer had surplus equipment to donate.

[33]The computer recyclers interviewed for this study were foundations or other 501(c)3 nonprofit organizations, although some for-profit firms also recycle and sell used computers.

whether it is in working order or repairable; replaces missing components; repairs, refurbishes and/or upgrades the equipment; and arranges delivery to the recipient. In addition to taking over some of the management functions, the recycler relieves the donor organization of the responsibility and cost of ensuring that donated computers are in good working order. Many, although not all, recyclers further warrantee or guarantee replacement of the equipment they transfer, typically for one year. Other organizations simply act as intermediaries and require donors to ensure the equipment is in working order.

Compared to the direct donation programs, recycling can increase the quantity and utility of the equipment ultimately transferred to a school. Because recyclers can use parts of nonworking or incomplete systems, this approach offers prospects for transferring larger numbers of used computers. Moreover, recyclers often can upgrade older computers into Internet-ready, multimedia units by adding more memory, faster processors, CD-ROM drives, and modems.

There are now literally thousands of computer donation or recycling programs in the United States, including a sizable listing on the World Wide Web.[34] They vary widely in their scale of operation, geographic scope, sources of equipment donations and funding, selection of recipients, and arrangements with recipients and other organizations. Most nonprofit recyclers are very small, but some handle thousands of computers annually. California, Indiana, and a few other states now provide state funds or other support for computer recycling to schools. Appendix B provides an indication of the different approaches some of the larger recycling organizations have used and contains brief descriptions of five recycling organizations and two other intermediary organizations interviewed for the study.

Because of the potential size of any federal donation program, the capacity of the recycling organization is important. What we found from looking at the details of several kinds of approaches was that, for a recycler to do substantial repair or upgrading, the organization must essentially operate a small business based on several essential elements: a regular supply of usable donated equipment; arrangements for equipment pickup and delivery; substantial warehouse and repair space; working capital, including funds to purchase parts and expendable supplies; skilled technical staff and/or trainers for volunteer or student refurbishers; and effective on-site management.

---

[34]A listing of recycling programs can be found on the Web (http://www.microweb.com/pepsite/Recycle/recycle_index.htm).

An organization missing any of these components will be limited in the extent of recycling it can accomplish. School vocational programs, for example, often lack discretionary funds to purchase new parts and supplies. They may be able to repair donated computers but be unable to upgrade them to meet current classroom needs. For example, the recyclers we interviewed said that upgrading a donated 386 computer to 486 or greater capability requires $200–300 in additional parts or components.

Lessons Learned from Past Programs

Our review of the experiences of both direct donor programs and the use of recyclers and intermediaries led to several conclusions that could inform the goals and implementation of E.O. 12999:

1. **Schools can benefit from donated computers.** While donations of used equipment should not replace funds for new purchases, they still can benefit the schools. Schools can make productive use of less-advanced machines for some applications, such as keyboarding and word processing, as well as administrative tasks. Donated equipment that has been refurbished can extend limited school budgets and accelerate the integration of educational technology into the classroom. Recyclers can upgrade less-advanced used computers for multimedia and Internet use for roughly one-third of the cost of an equivalent new machine.[35]

    Although the focus of this study is the implementation and best practices of the donors, it is important to note that the recipients, the schools, also play a role in making this an effective program. For schools to benefit from any donor program, they need a technology plan so that they can select and allocate both old and new computers to appropriate applications.

2. **Transferring equipment in good working order is essential.** Gifts of nonworking equipment are usually counterproductive for both donors and recipients, although school administrators often feel that, for political reasons, they cannot refuse computer donations from local businesses and donors. There is much anecdotal evidence that both private- and public-sector donations are often inoperable or incomplete. While some schools and districts have computer-repair capabilities through vocational classes,[36] the

---

[35]Recyclers typically use a 3/1 or 4/1 "rule of thumb" in deciding whether a donated machine should be refurbished or simply taken apart; that is, the system when transferred should be worth at least three or four times the cost of its repair and/or upgrading.

[36]For example, the San Diego Unified School District channels computer donations through its Regional Occupational Program, where students check out and repair the machines before they are placed in other classrooms.

majority of schools cannot use donations unless they are complete working systems.

3. **Donation programs must be managed.** Corporate and federal donation programs, regardless of size and strategy, were most effective when they received active senior management support; had clearly thought through objectives, approaches, and organizational implications; and had adequate staff time and other resources to meet the goal.

4. **Refurbishing provides more and better equipment for schools.** Recyclers told us that, at most, 25 to 35 percent of the donated computers they receive can be transferred as is.[37] If the recycler has funds to buy additional parts and missing components, the usable output can be doubled to 60 to 70 percent of incoming donations. Moreover, recyclers often warrantee and/or upgrade the computers transferred to the schools.

5. **Recycling organizations offer advantages, but other approaches to refurbishing also seem feasible.** Independent recycling organizations can operate at larger scale than can individual donors or recipients, but other models should be explored. These include vocational education programs run by school districts or other work-training approaches.[38]

Summary

Schools benefit the most from donated equipment that arrives in good working condition. Well-managed recycling programs have proven valuable in increasing the yield of workable computer systems that can be transferred to schools, as well as in refurbishing, upgrading, and warranting equipment. Intermediaries also offer advantages in that their participation may increase the willingness of private firms and agencies to make donations.

---

[37]The 25- to 35-percent range applies to recycling organizations that have minimum standards for computer donations. Other recyclers, such as the Computer Recycling Center in Santa Clara, CA, and the Lazarus Foundation in Baltimore, MD, will accept virtually any equipment donation and consequently have a lower percentage of systems that are operational as-is.

[38]The Los Angeles County Office of Education, for example, is working to establish community refurbishing partnerships that will train out-of-work and other low-income residents in computer repair skills. The U.S. Bureau of Prisons is piloting a recycling program as job training for prisoners.

5. Findings and Recommendations

The early stages of the implementation have involved two broad groups of departments and agencies. The first, consisting of the largest departments and agencies and those with missions emphasizing technology, have modified existing programs. The second group, consisting generally of smaller agencies with mission less oriented toward technology, have had to create new programs and policies. Naturally, the resulting picture is mixed, but in general, implementation seems to be proceeding in a reasonable fashion.

The following discussion summarizes our assessment of the potential contributions that activities under E.O. 12999 can make to K–12 education. We also identify key issues in the early implementation of the program and describe the characteristics of effective private and public donation programs. We conclude with recommendations for ways in which activities under E.O. 12999 and the E.O. itself might be improved.

Findings Concerning the Value of Surplus Federal Computers for Schools

Transfers under E.O. 12999 can make a useful contribution to the number of computers added to schools annually. We estimate that transfers in the first year of the program represented 3 to 4 percent of the computers schools acquired in 1996. That percentage could be significantly higher if the program used more of the computers we believe are available from federal agencies and federal contractors. While some of the schools, school systems, and experts we interviewed questioned the value of programs that donate used equipment to schools, the experiences of private sector, nonprofit programs, several state programs, and prior federal programs demonstrate that donated equipment can have value to schools if the equipment is prepared properly before delivery to the school and if the school possesses the understanding and capability to utilize the equipment appropriately.

The technological sophistication of the school is critical. Most computers made available through the program represent low-end technology and often need repair or upgrading to be useful educationally. Schools have limited capacities to install, maintain, repair, or upgrade computers. Low-end computers have limited applications. While these applications are educationally important, schools have many needs that cannot be served by donated equipment. This fact makes solid planning at the school and district levels essential for the effective use of this equipment. Anecdotal reports suggest that such planning is not yet common.

To deal with these realities, corporate donors are increasingly turning to recyclers. The use of recyclers can ensure that schools receive not only operable computers but upgraded equipment capable of running multimedia software and connecting classrooms to the Internet. Use of such intermediaries in the federal program could significantly increase both the number and quality of working computers transferred to schools and other qualified recipients.

Findings Concerning the Early Implementation of the E.O.

Federal agencies have responded to the E.O. by creating implementation plans, designating responsible offices, and devising reporting systems. Implementation has tended to be decentralized, reflecting the wide geographic dispersion of equipment covered by the E.O. However, several of the larger agencies and departments have retained some centralized control over the selection of recipients, in part to ensure that there is some equity in distribution of equipment among schools.

The level of effort by agencies varies according to agency characteristics. These include the size of computer inventories, the perceived congruence of the E.O. with agency missions, the nature of previous donation activities, staff resources in an era of downsizing, and the presence of committed individuals. Most successful implementations of this or earlier E.O.s owed their success to the initiative of such individuals. Implementation of E.O. 12999 should continue to recognize the importance of individual, local initiatives.

Potential federal intermediaries, such as the FEBs and GSA, have provided only sporadic, limited assistance. While the language of the E.O. suggests using FEBs to help link agencies and schools, and in a few regions the FEBs have facilitated the distribution of computers, the boards' organizational structure and limited staffing make them ill suited to fulfill this function over the long term. GSA could potentially provide such assistance, but only a few regional agency leaders have taken the initiative to do so.

The language of the E.O itself needs clarification. Federal agencies raised questions about relative priorities among program goals, recipient eligibility, and other aspects of the E.O. Many of their concerns focus on specific language in the E.O., such as:

- Do the words "supersede E.O. 12821" remove the authorization of some previous programs operating under slightly different guidance concerning what kind of equipment is transferred and whether employee time can be used for the program?

- Do the words "preference to" schools in EZs and ECs mean that other programs (such as those relating to an agency's mission or an existing partnership agreement) no longer receive priority?

- Does the language concerning *donation* versus *transfer*, and other aspects of the E.O., confuse the two different kinds of transfer authority under the Stevenson-Wydler Act and the Federal Property and Administrative Services Act?

An interagency working group is looking at ways to address these issues, which we expect can rather easily be resolved.

Widening the distribution of computers is a challenge. Because agencies cannot pack or ship the computers, distribution to schools may end up reflecting the geographic distribution of the donating agencies. For example, agencies find it difficult to transfer equipment to schools located in EZs and ECs both because of geographic distance and because contacts are limited in these areas. Transportation and outreach constraints favor aggressive and entrepreneurial schools grabbing the largest share of the computers.

In general, agencies have tried to ensure that donations do not go to only a few recipients. Agency policies assigning priorities among potential recipients and tracking which schools receive computers may help widen the distribution. Current efforts to enlist volunteer transportation may also help address this issue. However, given the comparatively low value of much of the equipment involved and its low volume relative to total school needs, it may not be worthwhile to expend too much effort to address this problem.

Findings Concerning Characteristics of Effective Donation Programs

There are many donation and recycling programs across the nation. Most are small and of uneven quality. However, a substantial number have had significant experience, and their operations provide important lessons for donation programs implemented under the guidance of E.O. 12999.

Donated equipment needs to arrive in good working order, unless the schools are willing to accept nonworking computers for repair by vocational classes. We have seen a number of effective programs that teach students to inspect, diagnose, and repair equipment, as well as install and maintain it in schools. Obviously, programs such as this have potential value for both the students and the schools. Where equipment is donated in operating condition, equipment warrantees or guaranteed replacement are also desirable.

Well-managed recycling programs have proven valuable in increasing the yield of workable computer systems that can be transferred to schools, as well as in refurbishing, upgrading, and warranting equipment. The experience of one large recycler suggests that such programs can effectively double the number of systems arriving at schools in operating condition, assuming the programs have a sufficient number of systems to manipulate nonworking computers into operating computers. Recycling programs have also provided opportunities for productive training and work for such groups as prison inmates or vocational students.

Some corporations have found intermediaries useful in reducing adverse publicity associated with donation programs. Intermediaries can help identify appropriate recipients and ensure that only operable equipment is transferred. Involving intermediaries—notably, recycling firms—may increase the willingness of private firms and agencies to make donations.

Recommendations

Our analysis leads to several recommendations, several of which we understand the interagency working group is attempting to address:.

1. The uncertainties surrounding the E.O. should be clarified for participating agencies. GSA should continue efforts to issue clear written guidance concerning the status of preexisting computer and research equipment transfer programs; the relative priority to be given to EZ/EC schools; and the eligibility of nonpublic, educational nonprofit organizations. The Executive Office of the President (EOP) should also consider directing GSA to draft model guidelines for donation programs that clarify these and other aspects of the E.O. and should also encourage local agency initiatives.

2. To make the program more beneficial for schools, federal agencies that make direct donations to schools should strive to transfer complete, working computer systems, unless schools have repair capabilities and are willing to accept partial systems or nonworking equipment.

3. To increase the quality and yield of donations, federal agencies should be permitted and encouraged to use qualified computer recycling and intermediary organizations. The EOP and GSA should determine whether legislative or administrative changes are needed to transfer federal equipment titles to recycling organizations that reassemble parts from several donations into upgraded working systems. Policymakers should also explore ways in which federal agencies can coordinate their efforts with state-sponsored or other recycling programs.

4. To maximize the usefulness of the computers to participating schools, federal policymakers and agencies should continue to improve the selection process among agency donors and school recipients. Expanding current efforts to use the Internet to exchange information about equipment supply and demand is one approach that deserves consideration.

5. The donation programs should continue to foster the local and regional initiative and personal commitment that appears to be associated with success. Overly cumbersome centralization or the use of centrally administered clearinghouses seems inappropriate.

In summary, the CTI believes that the efforts already under way and planned in response to E.O. 12999 are making useful contributions to the nation's schools. Implementing our recommendations can improve these contributions, particularly if the federal activities encourage, complement, and assist private and state programs. However, it is important to keep in mind that donation programs of the type encouraged by the E.O. can constitute only a small part of the national effort to equip schools and enable them to use technology to significantly improve student learning.

Appendix

A. Text of Executive Order 12999, *Educational Technology: Ensuring Opportunity for All Children in the Next Century*[39]

In order to ensure that American children have the skills they need to succeed in the information-intensive 21st century, the Federal Government is committed to working with the private sector to promote four major developments in American education: making modern computer technology an integral part of every classroom; providing teachers with the professional development they need to use new technologies effectively; connecting classrooms to the National Information Infrastructure; and encouraging the creation of excellent educational software. This Executive order streamlines the transfer of excess and surplus Federal computer equipment to our Nation's classrooms and encourages Federal employees to volunteer their time and expertise to assist teachers and to connect classrooms.

Accordingly, by the authority vested in me as President by the Constitution and the laws of the United States of America, including the provisions of the Stevenson-Wydler Technology Innovation Act of 1980, as amended (15 U.S.C. 3701 et seq.), the Federal Property and Administrative Services Act of 1949, ch. 288, 63 Stat. 377, and the National Defense Authorization Act for Fiscal Year 1996, Public Law 104-106, it is hereby ordered as follows:

Section 1. Protection of Educationally Useful Federal Equipment. (a) Educationally useful Federal equipment is a vital national resource. To the extent such equipment can be used as is, separated into parts for other computers, or upgraded—either by professional technicians, students, or other recycling efforts—educationally useful Federal equipment is a valuable tool for computer education. Therefore, to the extent possible, all executive departments and agencies (hereinafter referred to as "agencies") shall protect and safeguard such equipment, particularly when declared excess or surplus, so that it may be recycled and transferred, if appropriate, pursuant to this order.

---

[39]*Federal Register*: April 19, 1996 (Vol. 61, No. 77), pp. 17227–17229.

Sec. 2. Efficient Transfer of Educationally Useful Federal Equipment to Schools and Nonprofit Organizations. (a) To the extent permitted by law, all agencies shall give highest preference to schools and nonprofit organizations, including community-based educational organizations, ("schools and nonprofit organizations") in the transfer, through gift or donation, of educationally useful Federal equipment.

(b) Agencies shall attempt to give particular preference to schools and nonprofit organizations located in the Federal enterprise communities and empowerment zones established in the Omnibus Reconciliation Act of 1993, Public Law 103-66.

(c) Each agency shall, to the extent permitted by law and where appropriate, identify educationally useful Federal equipment that it no longer needs and transfer it to a school or nonprofit organization by:

(1) conveying research equipment directly to the school or organization pursuant to 15 U.S.C. 3710(i);or

(2) reporting excess equipment to the General Services Administration (GSA) for donation when declared surplus in accordance with section 203(j) of the Federal Property and Administrative Services Act of 1949, as amended, 40 U.S.C. 484(j). Agencies shall report such equipment as far as possible in advance of the date the equipment becomes excess, so that GSA may attempt to arrange direct transfers from the donating agency to recipients eligible under this order.

(d) In transfers made pursuant to paragraph (c)(1) of this section, title shall transfer directly from the agency to the schools or nonprofit organizations as required by 15 U.S.C. 3710(i). All such transfers shall be reported to the GSA. At the direction of the recipient institution or organization, and if appropriate, transferred equipment may be conveyed initially to a nonprofit reuse or recycling program that will upgrade it before transfer to the school or nonprofit organization holding title.

(e) All transfers to schools or nonprofit organizations, whether made directly or through GSA, shall be made at the lowest cost to the school or nonprofit organization permitted by law.

(f) The availability of educationally useful Federal equipment shall be made known to eligible recipients under this order by all practicable means, including newspaper, community announcements, and the Internet.

(g) The regional Federal Executive Boards shall help facilitate the transfer of educationally useful Federal equipment from the agencies they represent to recipients eligible under this order.

Sec. 3. Assisting Teachers' Professional Development: Connecting Classrooms. (a) Each agency that has employees who have computer expertise shall, to the extent permitted by law and in accordance with the guidelines of the Office of Personnel Management, encourage those employees to:

(1) help connect America's classrooms to the National Information Infrastructure;

(2) assist teachers in learning to use computers to teach; and

(3) provide ongoing maintenance of and technical support for the educationally useful Federal equipment transferred pursuant to this order.

(b) Each agency described in subsection (a) shall submit to the Office of Science and Technology Policy, within 6 months of the date of this order, an implementation plan to advance the developments described in this order, particularly those required in this section. The plan shall be consistent with approved agency budget totals and shall be coordinated through the Office of Science and Technology Policy.

(c) Nothing in this order shall be interpreted to bar a recipient of educationally useful Federal equipment from lending that equipment, whether on a permanent or temporary basis, to a teacher, administrator, student, employee, or other designated person in furtherance of educational goals.

Sec. 4. Definitions. For the purposes of this order:

(a) "Schools" means individual public or private education institutions encompassing prekindergarten through twelfth grade, as well as public school districts.

(b) "Community-based educational organizations" means nonprofit entities that are engaged in collaborative projects with schools or that have education as their primary focus. Such organizations shall qualify as nonprofit educational institutions or organizations for purposes of section 203(j) of the Federal Property and Administrative Services Act of 1949, as amended.

(c) "Educationally useful Federal equipment" means computers and related peripheral tools (e.g., printers, modems, routers, and servers), including telecommunications and research equipment, that are appropriate for use in prekindergarten, elementary, middle, or secondary school education. It shall also include computer software, where the transfer of licenses is permitted.

(d) "Nonprofit reuse or recycling program" means a 501(c) organization able to upgrade computer equipment at no or low cost to the school or nonprofit organization taking title to it.

(e) "Federal Executive Boards," as defined in 5 C.F.R. Part 960, are regional organizations of each Federal agency's highest local officials.

Sec. 5. This order shall supersede Executive Order No.12821 of November 16, 1992.

Sec. 6. Judicial Review. This order is not intended, and should not be construed, to create any right or benefit, substantive or procedural, enforceable at law by a party against the United States, its agencies, its officers, or its employees.

(Presidential Sig.)

THE WHITE HOUSE,
    April 17, 1996.

[FR Doc. 96-9866
Filed 4-18-96; 8:45 am]

B. Brief Descriptions of Selected Recycling and Intermediary Organizations

The **Detwiler Foundation**, founded in 1991 to facilitate computer donations to schools in California, has become the nation's largest computer recycling program. In 1996, the foundation arranged for transfer to schools of some 17,000 computers, most of which were refurbished by California prison inmates with state funds from a new $10 million California Computer Refurbishing Fund. Detwiler receives most of its operating support and equipment donations from large corporations in California. The foundation has set minimum standards (currently 386 or better for Internet access; 486 or better for curriculum applications) for donations, but it will take nonworking computers, which are either repaired or cannibalized for parts. The refurbished and often upgraded computers are then transferred to schools at no cost, with a one-year replacement guarantee.

Donors may specify recipients and the method of distribution. However, the Detwiler Foundation encourages donors to adopt a "Matching Challenge" requirement in which schools match the computers they receive on a one-to-one basis with donations from other sources. This is one of the more controversial aspects of the Detwiler program, because schools must obtain their matches from non-Detwiler sources (i.e., mostly from small companies and individuals), and the foundation does not refurbish or guarantee replacement of the matching computers. Other issues raised by educators about the Detwiler program include its political visibility and its potential to displace state and local funds for new technology purchases. Still, there appears to be high demand by schools for the recycled equipment, and the Detwiler Foundation is now probably the largest supplier of computers to K–12 schools in California. The foundation is expanding its recycling program to other states.

The **Computer Recycling Center** is a nonprofit organization based in Santa Clara, California. It accepts computer equipment of all sorts and in any condition from a wide range of individual and corporate donors. Using some paid staff and about 150 volunteers at its three sites in Northern California, the Center has refurbished an estimated 25,000 computers in the past three years for K–12 schools in California and neighboring states. Recipients pay only for delivery charges. Donors may specify recipients, although the center prefers to make the determination according to need and intended application. With expanded facilities and a recent $2.9 million grant from the California Computer Refurbishing Fund, the center expects to increase its scale and scope of operations in 1997.

The Computer Recycling Center incorporates some unique approaches to recycling computers and transferring them to schools. To maximize the quantity of like equipment it transfers, the Center buys scrap computers in bulk from corporate liquidators. Donated or purchased equipment that is unusable for schools is either sold to the general public or further dismantled, sorted, and sold as scrap materials. Funds from these sales are used to support the center's programs. The center also goes beyond simply giving used computers to schools by assisting schools to develop technology plans and providing training, materials, and other support for school vocational repair programs. The Computer Recycling Center is certified by the State of California to provide vocational training in computer repair.

The **Indiana Buddy Up Program** is a self-financed state program established in 1992 to refurbish donated used computers and resell them at cost to K–12 schools in Indiana. It is operated by the Indiana State Board of Education, the nonprofit Corporation for Educational Technology, and the state's nine Educational Service Centers. Donors receive a special $125 state tax credit for computers in working condition that meet minimum Buddy Up requirements (currently 386 or 68030 processor, or better). Minor repairs and upgrades (e.g., adding more memory or a color monitor) are made by paid staff at the Central Indiana Educational Service Center, and the computers are loaded with Windows and Microsoft Works software, for which the program has a wholesale license. The service centers send regular mailings to schools describing the recycled computers that are available and also lists them on the Internet.[40] Schools can purchase them at cost—currently, $395–435, which includes parts, labor, program administration, and the $125 tax credit. Donors cannot select the recipients. The Buddy Up program initially was intended to offer recycled computers to parents as well as to schools, but so far the demand from schools has exceeded the available supply.

The **East-West Education Development Foundation** in Boston, Massachusetts, was established in 1990 to send used computers to democracy and human-rights organizations in the former Soviet Union but now distributes 70 percent of its output to schools and nonprofit organizations in the United States. It expects to

---

[40]On the World Wide Web at http://www.doe.state.in.us/olr/

place about 5,000 remanufactured computers with U.S. recipients in 1997. The foundation will accept all computer donations from individuals or corporations. It remanufactures computers at its own facility, using both paid staff and volunteers (each remanufactured computer requires about four donated machines, according to the marketing director). Excess materials are sold as scrap, and the computers are provided at cost—currently $50 for a 286, $150 for a 386, $325 for a 486, and $690 for a 586 or Pentium-class machine. The foundation has a large waiting list of interested recipients throughout the United States, split roughly 50-50 between schools and other nonprofits. Donors can specify the recipients if they pay for the refurbishing costs. In some cases, East-West will assist recipients in finding sponsors to cover these costs.

Although the **Lazarus Foundation** operates at a smaller scale than the previously described recyclers, it is included because it has worked with federal agencies in the Baltimore, Maryland, and suburban Washington, D.C., areas. The foundation accepts donations of 286 or better computer equipment in any condition—more than 50 percent of the computers it received in 1996 had 286 processors. Volunteers meet once a month in donated shop space in Columbia, Maryland, to repair the donated machines, which are then resold at cost (an average $300 for an upgraded 386) to schools and nonprofits. In 1996, the foundation cohosted a "National Computer Recycling Conference," which a number of federal employees attended. It also sponsored a "Tech Day" aimed at recycling computers for schools in the Baltimore Empowerment Zone. Federal agencies donated about 400 used computers for the Baltimore Tech Day, of which about 125 were refurbished at no charge and the rest given as-is to the Baltimore School System.

Gifts In Kind acts as an intermediary for corporations that want to donate manufactured products to nonprofits and schools. The organization deals mostly with new-product donations (valued at a total of $250 million in 1996), but since 1990 it has also warehoused and distributed used computers. The computers must be in good working condition; Gifts In Kind does no inspection, repair, or refurbishing. Gifts In Kind helps donors identify appropriate recipients in accordance with the donor's specifications. It maintains a register of some 50,000 qualified recipients, mails them a monthly listing of the equipment it has available, and processes requests and shipments. If donors do not pay shipping costs, it charges recipients a nominal fee ($75) for shipping and handling. Although it has not aggressively marketed recycled computers, Gifts In Kind estimates it has distributed about 10,000 used computers in the past three years and expects to double that number in 1997. About 25 percent of the used computers have gone to schools.

The **National Cristina Foundation** also links donors of used computer equipment with school and nonprofit recipients. It sees its roles as helping recipients define their technology needs and share solutions, facilitating communications between donors and recipients, and keeping track of the equipment transfers. Its guidelines for donors do not require refurbishing or warrantees, but state that all equipment must be "usable." National Cristina maintains a register of qualified recipients, about half of which are schools; it channels some donations through community recycling programs. National Cristina expects to broker some 30,000 donated items—mostly computers, but also peripherals, and related equipment—in 1997.

Table B.1

Recycling and Intermediary Program Comparisons

Recycling or Intermediary Organization	Estimated No. to Be Placed in 1997	Refurbishing Done By	Equipment Warrantee	Principal Recipients	Recipient Pays Costs?
Detwiler Foundation/ Calif. Reburbishing Fund	30,000	State prisoners	1 year	CA schools	No
Computer Recycling Ctr/ Calif. Reburbishing Fund	15,000	Paid staff & volunteers	1 year	CA schools	No
Buddy Up Program, Indiana	3,000	Paid staff	1 year	IN schools	Yes
East-West Education Development Foundation	5,000	Paid staff & volunteers	4 months	Schools, nonprofits	Yes
Lazarus Foundation	<1,000	Volunteers	Varies	MD schools, nonprofits	Yes
Gifts in Kind	20,000	None	None	U.S. schools, nonprofits	$75
National Cristina Foundation	30,000	None	None	U.S. schools, nonprofits	No